No Backbone!
The World of Invertebrates

Roly-Poly Pillbugs

by Molly Smith

Consultant: Patricia S. Sadeghian
Associate Curator of Invertebrate Zoology
Santa Barbara Museum of Natural History

BEARPORT
PUBLISHING

NEW YORK, NEW YORK

Credits

Cover, © Mitsuhiko Imamori/Minden Pictures/FLPA and © Dwight Kuhn/Dwight Kuhn Photography; TOC, © Ted Kinsman/Kinsman Physics Productions/Photolibrary; 4, © Mitsuhiko Imamori/Minden Pictures; 6T, © Lynette Schimming; 6C, © Asankowski/F1 Online/Photolibrary; 6B, © EcoPrint/Shutterstock; 7, © Roger Steene/Image Quest Marine; 8, © Mitsuhiko Imamori/Minden Pictures; 9, © Dwight Kuhn/Dwight Kuhn Photography; 11, © Nature Production/Nature Picture Library; 12T, © James P. Rowan; 12B, © Dwight Kuhn/Dwight Kuhn Photography; 13, © Mitsuhiko Imamori/Minden Pictures; 14T, © Dwight Kuhn/Dwight Kuhn Photography; 14B, © Dwight Kuhn/Dwight Kuhn Photography; 15, © Dwight Kuhn/Dwight Kuhn Photography; 16, © Nature Production/Nature Picture Library; 17, © Mitsuhiko Imamori/Minden Pictures; 18T, © Stephen Dalton/NHPA/Photoshot; 18C, © Mitsuhiko Imamori/Minden Pictures; 18B, © Mitsuhiko Imamori/Minden Pictures/FLPA; 19, © John Devries/Tips Italia/Photolibrary; 20, © Lynette Schimming; 21, © Mitsuhiko Imamori/Minden Pictures/FLPA; 22TL, © Zigmund Leszczynski/Photolibrary; 22TR, © Asankowski/F1 Online/Photolibrary; 22BL, © Dwight Kuhn/Dwight Kuhn Photography; 22BR, © Kimberly Ann Reinick/Shutterstock; 22Spot, © Joseph Calev/iStockphoto; 23TL, © Dwight Kuhn/Dwight Kuhn Photography; 23TR, © Jim Wehtje/Photodisc/Getty Images; 23BL, © Kurt_G/Shutterstock; 23BR, © Joseph Calev/Shutterstock; 24, © arlindo71/iStockphoto.

Publisher: Kenn Goin
Editorial Director: Adam Siegel
Creative Director: Spencer Brinker
Original Design: Dawn Beard Creative
Photo Researcher: Q2A Media: Poulomi Basu

Library of Congress Cataloging-in-Publication Data

Smith, Molly, 1974–
  Roly-poly pillbugs / by Molly Smith.
    p. cm. — (No backbone! The world of invertebrates)
  Includes bibliographical references.
  ISBN-13: 978-1-59716-754-3 (library binding)
  ISBN-10: 1-59716-754-1 (library binding)
  1. Wood lice (Crustaceans)—Juvenile literature. I. Title.

QL444.M34S65 2009
595.3'72—dc22

                        2008042378

For more information, write to Bearport Publishing Company, Inc., 45 West 21st Street, Suite 3B, New York, New York 10010. Printed in the United States of America.

10 9 8 7 6 5 4

Contents

Roly-Polies

Pillbugs are small brownish-gray creatures that are shaped like ovals.

Sometimes they roll up into a ball to protect themselves.

When they do, they look like little round pills.

In fact, that's how they got their name.

On Land and in the Sea

pillbug

Many people think that pillbugs are **insects**—just like ants, bees, and beetles.

These little creepy-crawlers are not insects, however.

shrimp

Instead, they belong to a large group of animals that includes shrimp, lobsters, and crabs.

Most of the animals in this group live underwater.

Pillbugs, however, live on land.

crab

A Pillbug's Body

There are about 4,000 kinds of pillbugs.

Most are about one-half inch (1.27 cm) long.

All of them have three main body parts—a head, a middle part, and an end part called the abdomen.

All of their bodies also have a covering called an exoskeleton.

The top part of the exoskeleton is made up of hard, thick plates.

8

seven segments

abdomen

Insects have three pairs of legs. Pillbugs, however, have seven pairs. They are attached to seven **segments** in the middle of a pillbug's body.

head

legs

middle part

9

Damp, Dark Homes

Crabs, lobsters, and other relatives of the pillbug use body parts called gills to breathe underwater.

Pillbugs also use gills to breathe—but they use them on land.

To do so, they have to stay only in wet, moist places.

Rotting logs and piles of rocks or leaves are some of the dark, damp spots where pillbugs live.

Some pillbugs dig into the ground to stay moist.

Leaves and Logs for Dinner

In the cool of the night, pillbugs come out to look for food.

They mainly eat parts of dead plants.

They are often found chewing on fallen leaves or rotting logs.

Sometimes pillbugs eat parts of living plants, too.

A pillbug has a large pair of **antennas** on its head that it uses for feeling and smelling. The antennas help the pillbug find its food.

antennas

13

A Pouch Full of Pillbugs

Just like adult pillbugs, baby pillbugs need water to live.

They start out as eggs, protected in a watery pouch that a mother pillbug carries under her body.

After a few weeks, the eggs hatch inside the pouch.

The baby pillbugs stay in the pouch for another few weeks.

Then they are ready to start living on land.

eggs

baby pillbugs in pouch

A mother pillbug can carry up to 200 eggs in her pouch.

14

baby pillbugs leaving pouch

Growing Up

A baby pillbug looks like a tiny, white adult.

While it is growing to full size, it sheds its old exoskeleton and forms a new, bigger one several times.

This change is called molting.

With each molt, the pillbug becomes darker.

At first, a baby pillbug has only six pairs of legs. It grows its seventh pair after it molts for the first time.

old exoskeleton

baby pillbug

adult pillbug

baby pillbugs

17

Staying Safe

Spiders, lizards, frogs, birds, and shrews all like to eat pillbugs.

Luckily, a pillbug has ways of staying safe from these enemies.

Its dull color blends in with the earth and helps it stay hidden.

If a pillbug is still found by an enemy, it can roll up into a ball to protect the softer parts of its body.

The hard plates on the pillbug's covering make it hard for the enemy to bite into it.

spider

lizard

frog

shrew

Some pillbugs can release a liquid that smells and tastes bad to enemies.

Winter Homes

Pillbugs do not like cold weather.

The ones that live in cold places make burrows for the winter.

These homes may be in logs, under old boards, or even in buildings.

The pillbugs go to sleep inside them.

They stay in their burrows during the winter.

In the spring, they come back out and return to their roly-poly lives.

pillbugs during winter

Most pillbugs live for about two years. Some can live as long as five years.

A World of Invertebrates

An animal that has a skeleton with a **backbone** inside its body is a *vertebrate* (VUR-tuh-brit). Mammals, birds, fish, reptiles, and amphibians are all vertebrates.

An animal that does not have a skeleton with a backbone inside its body is an *invertebrate* (in-VUR-tuh-brit). More than 95 percent of all kinds of animals on Earth are invertebrates.

Some invertebrates, such as insects and spiders, have hard skeletons—called exoskeletons—on the outside of their bodies. Other invertebrates, such as worms and jellyfish, have soft, squishy bodies with no exoskeletons to protect them.

Here are four animals that are related to pillbugs. Like pillbugs, they are all invertebrates.

Lobster

Shrimp

Crayfish

Crab

Glossary

antennas
(an-TEN-uhz)
the long, thin
body parts on
a pillbug's head
used for feeling
and smelling

backbone
(BAK-bohn)
a group of
connected bones
that run along
the backs of some
animals, such as
dogs, cats, and fish;
also called a spine

insects
(IN-sekts) small
animals that have
six legs, three
main body parts,
two antennas,
and a hard
covering called an
exoskeleton

segments
(SEG-muhnts)
strip-shaped parts
of a pillbug's body

Index

Read More

Himmelman, John. *A Pill Bug's Life.* New York: Children's Press (1999).

Pyers, Greg. *Pill Bugs Up Close.* Chicago: Raintree (2005).

St. Pierre, Stephanie. *Pillbug.* Chicago: Heinemann Library (2008).

Learn More Online

To learn more about pillbugs, visit

www.bearportpublishing.com/NoBackbone–CreepyCrawlers

About the Author

Molly Smith has written many nonfiction books and textbooks for children. She lives with her husband and two daughters in Norwalk, Connecticut, where they like to hunt for pillbugs by their stone wall.